Drawing Is Fun!

DRAWING
SPORTS FIGURES

FRANKLIN WATTS
LONDON•SYDNEY

First published in 2012 by Franklin Watts

Copyright © 2012 Arcturus Publishing Limited

Franklin Watts
338 Euston Road
London NW1 3BH

Franklin Watts Australia
Level 17/207 Kent Street, Sydney NSW 2000

Produced by Arcturus Publishing Limited,
26/27 Bickels Yard, 151–153 Bermondsey Street, London SE1 3HA

The rights of Trevor Cook and Lisa Miles to be identified as the authors of this work have been asserted by them in accordance with the Copyright, Designs and Patents Act 1988.

Artwork: Q2A India
Text: Trevor Cook and Lisa Miles
Editors: Fiona Tulloch and Joe Harris
Cover design: Akihiro Nakayama

Picture credits: All photographs supplied by Shutterstock; except pages 24, 28 and 30, supplied by iStockphoto; and page 26 supplied by photos.com.

A CIP catalogue record for this book is available from the British Library.

Dewey Decimal Classification Number 743.8'97960922

ISBN 978 1 4451 1025 7

Printed in China

Franklin Watts is a division of Hachette Children's Books, an Hachette UK company.
www.hachette.co.uk

SL001765EN
Supplier 03, Date 0112, Print Run 1433

Contents

Gymnast 4-5

Ballet dancer 6-7

Horse rider 8-9

Skateboarder 10-11

Hang glider 12-13

Ice skater 14-15

Windsurfer 16-17

Roller skater 18-19

Tennis player 20-21

Football player 22-23

Baseball player 24-25

Deep-sea diver 26-27

Boxer 28-29

Flamenco dancer 30-31

Glossary and index 32

Gymnast

In gymnastics, people do special exercises.

The moves are hard. She makes them look easy.

She must practise every day.

She stands on one leg to do this exercise.

FUN FACTS ● FUN FACTS ● FUN FACTS ● FUN FACTS ● FUN FACTS

The first gymnasts lived in Greece more than two thousand years ago!

1. This shape is the body and the head.

2. One arm is reaching up.

3. She balances on her toes.

4. Her other leg is raised high behind her.

Ballet dancer

Ballet is a type of dance. The dancer makes it look beautiful.

The dancer needs strong arms and legs.

This ballet skirt is called a tutu.

She dances on the tips of her toes.

FUN FACTS ● FUN FACTS ● FUN FACTS ● FUN FACTS ● FUN FACTS

Dancers wear out ballet shoes very quickly. Some dancers get through two pairs each week!

1. Draw her graceful body and pretty skirt.

2. Her hair is put up in a bun.

3. Her arms are held out wide to help her balance.

4. She balances tall on one leg.

Horse rider

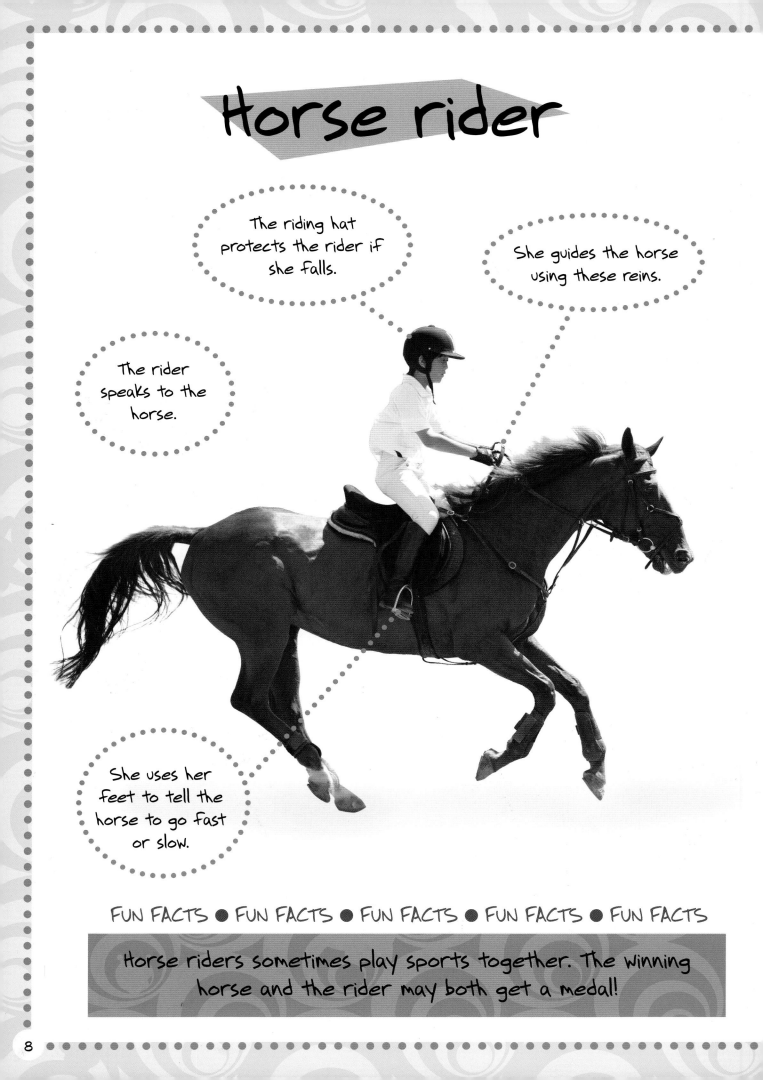

The riding hat protects the rider if she falls.

She guides the horse using these reins.

The rider speaks to the horse.

She uses her feet to tell the horse to go fast or slow.

FUN FACTS ● FUN FACTS ● FUN FACTS ● FUN FACTS ● FUN FACTS

Horse riders sometimes play sports together. The winning horse and the rider may both get a medal!

1. Draw the horse's body and the rider's body.

2. Give the rider a hat. Start the horse's legs.

3. Now draw the other two legs.

4. Make the horse and the rider smile.

Skateboarder

Skateboards can go very fast!

A skater can do tricks. He makes the board jump into the air.

He wears skate shoes and baggy clothes. These clothes let him move easily.

The top of the skateboard is rough. It helps the skater stay on.

FUN FACTS ● FUN FACTS ● FUN FACTS ● FUN FACTS ● FUN FACTS

Skateboarding was started by surfers. They wanted something to do when there were no waves!

1. Draw a head with a hat and a body.

2. Put in two strong legs.

3. Add his arms to help him balance.

4. Finish off with some pads on his elbows and knees.

Hang glider

A hang glider is like a huge kite. It has one big wing.

The wind lifts it into the air.

The person flying the hang glider is called the pilot.

He makes the hang glider take off. He runs then jumps into the air.

FUN FACTS ● FUN FACTS ● FUN FACTS ● FUN FACTS ● FUN FACTS

Pilots can fly in their hang gliders for hours. They can travel hundreds of kilometres!

1. Draw the big wing.

2. There's a bar hanging
   underneath.

3. Give him a helmet to
   keep him safe.

4. He guides the glider by
   holding the bar in front.

Ice skater

An ice skater dances on ice.

The skater's arms and legs make pretty shapes.

She skates to music. She has to keep time.

Ice skates help the skater to spin and jump.

FUN FACTS ● FUN FACTS ● FUN FACTS ● FUN FACTS ● FUN FACTS

Some ice skaters dance on ice. Others have races or play a game called ice hockey!

1. Draw her two arms first.

2. Now add her head with her hair flying up.

3. She's skating on one leg.

4. Give her a short skirt with lots of pleats.

Windsurfer

The wind blows the windsurfer across the water.

The sail traps the wind. It pushes the board along.

He has to know where the wind is coming from.

A windsurfer can do tricks. He can also take part in races.

FUN FACTS ● FUN FACTS ● FUN FACTS ● FUN FACTS ● FUN FACTS

Some people windsurf on indoor pools.
Big fans make the wind!

1. Two long shapes form the board and the mast.

2. The hands hold a bar.

3. Make his legs bend.

4. The sails are always colourful.

Roller skater

This skater wears a helmet on his head.

Some skates have two wheels at the front and two at the back.

These are called inline skates. The wheels are in a line.

He wears pads on his knees.

FUN FACTS ● FUN FACTS ● FUN FACTS ● FUN FACTS ● FUN FACTS

Roller skates were first used in a play in London, more than 250 years ago!

1. His body's quite thin.

2. He has long legs.

3. Draw his arms spread out for balance.

4. Give him elbow pads and a helmet in case he falls.

Tennis player

A tennis player hits the ball with a bat called a racket.

He can hit the ball soft or hard.

He hits the ball over a net.

Tennis shoes help him turn and run fast.

FUN FACTS ● FUN FACTS ● FUN FACTS ● FUN FACTS ● FUN FACTS

Some players hit the ball very hard. It travels twice as fast as a car on a motorway!

1. Here's his body and head.

2. Now put in his arms and hands.

3. He's reaching up to serve the ball.

4. He dresses mostly in white.

Football player

A football player plays on a team. There are 11 people in his team.

He can't touch the ball with his hands or arms.

Each team has a colour. The player wears it on his shirt and shorts.

Special football boots help him to run and kick.

FUN FACTS ● FUN FACTS ● FUN FACTS ● FUN FACTS ● FUN FACTS

Football is the most popular ball game in the world.

1. Draw the body first.

2. Put on his head and arms.

3. He is running fast.

4. Don't forget the ball!

Baseball player

A baseball player wears a cap. It keeps the sun out of his eyes.

This player is a hitter. He holds a baseball bat.

His uniform shows the colours of his team.

The player who throws the ball is called the pitcher.

FUN FACTS ● FUN FACTS ● FUN FACTS ● FUN FACTS ● FUN FACTS

The longest baseball game ever lasted eight hours!

1. Draw his arms and the top of his body.

2. Add his head.

3. Put in his long legs.

4. He's just hit the ball!

Deep-sea diver

The diver wears these flippers on his feet. They help him swim fast.

He carries a tank on his back. The tank is full of air.

He can stay under the water for around an hour.

He wears a wetsuit. It stops him from getting cold.

FUN FACTS ● FUN FACTS ● FUN FACTS ● FUN FACTS ● FUN FACTS

Some divers don't wear air tanks. They are called free divers. Free divers can hold their breath for a long time.

1. Draw the body and helmet.

2. Next put on the arms.

3. He's got gloves and flippers.

4. He has his own air in a tank on his back.

Boxer

A boxer has to be strong and quick.

He wears padded gloves. The gloves stop his hands from being hurt.

He wears baggy shorts so that he can move quickly and easily.

Boxing is a sport where two fighters hit each other.

FUN FACTS ● FUN FACTS ● FUN FACTS ● FUN FACTS ● FUN FACTS

Boxers fight other boxers that weigh the same.
A really huge boxer can't fight a tiny one!

1. Two shapes make the head and the body.

2. He's punching with his right fist.

3. He's wearing big gloves.

4. He has a helmet to protect his head.

Flamenco dancer

Flamenco is a fast type of dance.

The dancer moves her arms. She claps her hands and stamps her feet.

She shows a lot of feeling when she dances. There is happiness and sadness in the song.

Her shoes make loud stomping sounds on the floor.

FUN FACTS ● FUN FACTS ● FUN FACTS ● FUN FACTS ● FUN FACTS

Sometimes the dancer makes up the steps as she dances. She doesn't practise them first!

1. Draw her head and graceful arms.

2. Add her skirt and face.

3. Give the skirt swirls.

4. A pretty red trim finishes her skirt.

Glossary

baggy hanging in a loose way

balance stand or move without falling over

flipper a long, flat shoe that helps you to swim quickly. Also called 'fins'

graceful a pretty way of moving

helmet a kind of hat you wear to stop you hurting your head

highway a fast road between cities, such as a motorway

mast a pole that a sail is fixed to

pads these protect your elbows and knees if you fall

pilot someone who guides a plane or hang glider

racket a type of bat with a long handle. It has a round part at the end with strings across it.

reins a rider holds these and uses them to guide a horse

surfer someone who stands on a board and rides waves at the beach

tank something that is filled with a liquid, such as water, or a gas, such as air

tutu a pleated net skirt worn by ballet dancers

Further Reading

Explore and Draw Extreme Sports by Monica Halpern (Rourke Publishing, 2010)

How to Draw Faces by Barbara Levy Soloff (Dover Publications, 2003)

How to Draw Sports by Barbara Soloff Levy (Dover Publications, 2009)

Websites

How to draw sports:
http://www.dragoart.com/sports-c379-1.htm

How to draw a scuba diver:
drawinz.com/how_to/scuba-diver/

How to draw figures:
http://www.artyness.co.uk/figure-drawing.html

Index

A

Arms 5, 6, 7, 11, 14, 15, 19, 21, 23, 25, 27, 31

B

Ball 14, 20, 21, 22, 23, 24, 25

Ballet 6–7

Baseball 24–25

Bat 20, 24

Boxer 28–29

D

Dancing 6–7, 14, 30–31

F

Flamenco 30–31

Flippers 26, 27

Football 22–23

G

Gloves 27, 28, 29

Gymnast 4–5

H

Hang glider 12–13

Helmet 13, 18, 19, 27

Horse 8–9

I

Ice skates 14–15

L

Legs 4, 5, 6, 7, 9, 11, 15, 17, 19, 25

M

Mast 17

R

Roller skates 18–19

S

Sail 17

Scuba diver 26–27

Skateboard 10–11

Skirt 6, 7

T

Tennis 20–21

Toes 5, 6

Tutu 6

W

Wind 12, 16

Windsurfer 16–17